To Karen:

Who should've known, when that dog barked at her 2 year-old, and her daughter barked back, that no bitch was ever gonna play her kid.

Hickory Dickory Dock

I Do Not Want Your C*ck

A Book About Patriarchy

For Manchildren

Poems and Not-So-Great Illustrations by Kyla Jenée Lacey

Hickory Dickory Dock

Hickory Dickory Dock.

I do not want your cock.

The clock struck one,

Your pants are undone,

Hickory Dickory Dock.

Hickory Dickory Dock,

I do not want your cock.

The clock struck two,

I'm over you.

Hickory Dickory Dock.

Hickory Dickory Dock,

I do not want your cock.

The clock struck three,

Get away from me!

Hickory Dickory Dock.

Hickory Dickory Dock,

I do not want your cock.

The clock struck four,

I'm out the door,

Hickory Dickory Dock,

I do not want your cock,

The clock struck five,

My uber's arrived.

Hickory Dickory Dock

Hickory Dickory Dock

I do not want your cock

The clock struck seven,

Do I really have to count to eleven?

Hickory Dickory Dock

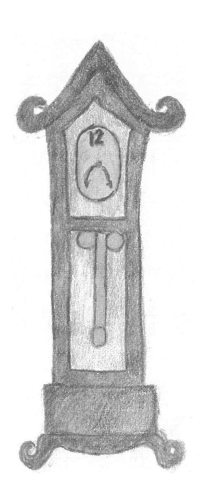

Hickory Dickory Dock

I do not want your cock.

The clock struck twelve,

Please go to hell!!

Hickory Dickory Dock.

Hickory Dickory Dock

Why scamper asked the cock?

You've scared me so,

I have to go!

Hickory Dickory BLOCKED!!!

If You Give A Man Your Cookie

If you give a man your cookie,

He might call you a whore,

He'll tell all his friends,

But wanna do it again,

He'll probably come back for more.

If you give a man your cookie,

He might not return your calls,

He will probably ignore you,

But then tell you he adores you

As soon as you've moved on.

If you give a man your cookie,

He might try to move in,

He might bring you bed bugs

And bring you bad vibes

From where he was previously living in.

If you give a man your cookie,

He might not act the same,

So ride that dick,

enjoy that shit,

Fuck him, just as long as YOU came!

WHAt diD yoU do to Make hiM hit yOu?

Can you imagine the indignation?

Of someone looking me dead in my face

And having the gall to pose the query,

What did I do to make him hit me.

To watch my life flash before my eyes,

But the blame on me, is what they surmise.

They say there's no such thing as a stupid question,

But if there were, this would be in that section.

I was a makeup artist to cover the bruises,

A clothing designer to cover contusions,

A really good storyteller to cover the truth,

What more could I possibly do?

If I am an adult, and so is he?

Then why do I have to take the culpability?

That if we are all in control of our own selves

Then why place the blame on someone else?

After you've braved such misery,

For someone to then imply your complicity,

Well if you really wanna know what I did to make him beat me up,

The answer is quite simple, Bitch, I didn't duck!

Fellati....NO!

If I gave you head,

You would surely just deceive me.

I would ask for the pleasure in return,

And you would pretend you're sleeping.

If I gave you head,

You would complain about my hair.

You would forget the fact that I brave the sweaty jungle,

Also known as your "Down there."

If I gave you head,

I would surely do my best,

I would get real nasty, do it right,

Even let you come on my chest.

But if you gave me head,

It would surely be a fight

And I don't wanna argue,

So I'm closing MY mouth, good night.

Hungry....Why Wait?

What did you do before we met,

How did you not starve to death?

What do you do when I'm not there?

Do you sit alone with cupboard bare?

What if I told you that you too could make dinner;

That the kitchen doesn't discriminate against gender.

What if I told you that the stove still works,

For nice guys and even for jerks.

What if I told you that you could cook;

That you could even learn how, from a book.

That you could be a culinary artist,

Instead of one who's just starving.

What if I told you that you could eat,

Without food prepared by me,

That you could do it without hesitation,

Even if you're only making....... reservations.

Bloody Hell

Just twelve days out the year, could you cater to me?
Bring me chocolate, the remote, and also rub my feet.
I don't know why you hate when I'm on my period,
Cause surely you'd cry the most, if I were to miss one.

I'm on my period, but YOU'RE the one fussy,
Just go the store please, and stop acting like a pussy
Cause I can guarantee that the pain of getting me pads
Doesn't hurt as much as these cramps.

Plus you don't have to worry if every sneeze,
Will have blood dripping down to your knees.
And even after decades of practicing,
You are still prone to accidents.

You don't have to bear this pain,

Just so you can bear children.

And that's not even a guarantee,

Because I can still get a period, with no fertility.

Every month I go through this turmoil!

So how in the hell is this not "normal"?

My ovaries are strong and endure more than their share,

So maybe YOU should grow a pair.

And when it's all said and done,

And I turn about 51,

And I'm almost done with commas, periods, and dashes,

Just my luck, "oh look, it's hot flashes!"

How Many Dicks Does It Take To Get To The Center Of The Hoe?

How many dicks does one have to take,

For her an actual hoe to make?

Does she have to have two at a time,

To be considered a hoe in her prime?

What is the difference between 1 dick thirty times,

Than 30 dicks once each in a line?

And how will it even destroy her walls?

If your small dick doesn't touch them at all?

Cause god forbid a girl enjoys,

The same sex she has with a boy,

Cause I'm sure your selfish ass is used to,

Being the only one that sex is good to,

I'm sorry you're not in anyone's top five lists

It's not that their pussies are an abyss,

That you conclude that's why someone's a hoe,

But rather that your dick is just abysmal,

Cause If I ask, how many dicks does a girl have to slumber?

To be a hoe, no one can give me a number.

But instead a mindset will be what you say,

Even if the woman doesn't think she's that way.

And why can't you just wash off your hoe?

And if it's so easily caught, then why is it so?

That it seems to be something sexually transmitted,

But men who fuck everything never seem to get it.

I was not asking for it in a house,

I was not asking for him to undo my blouse,
I was not asking for him to use his hand,

I was not asking to be raped by that man.

I was not asking for it with those shoes,

I was not asking for it drinking booze,

I was not asking for him to use his hand,

I was not asking to be raped by that man.

I was not asking for it with a flirt,

I was not asking for it with a skirt,

I was not asking for him to use his hand.

I was not asking to be raped by that man.

I was not asking for it with dinner and a date,

I was not asking because I stayed over late,

I was not asking for him to use his hand,

I was not asking to be raped by that man.

I was not asking because we had sex before,

I was not asking because you think I'm a whore.

I was not asking for him to use his hand,

I was not asking to be raped by that man.

I was not asking because we are dating,

I was not asking because you've been patiently waiting,

I was not asking for him to use his hand,

I was not asking to be raped by that man.

 I was not asking in the car,

I was not asking at the bar,

I was not asking for him to use his hand,

I was not asking to be raped by that man.

I was not asking because I was in shock,

I was not asking because I didn't scream stop,

I was not asking for him to use his hand,

I was not asking to be raped by that man.

I was not asking as a woman, not asking as a child,

I was not asking in a halter top, or a even flower night gown.

I was not asking for him to use his hand,

I was not asking to be raped by that man.

I was not asking for it while asleep,

I was not asking for it drunk in his jeep.

I was not asking for him to force my hand,

I was not asking to be raped by that man.

A,B,C, 1,2, 3SOME

You say you want a threesome,

I'm here to be your grace,

Even allowing you to cheat on me,

Right in my fucking face.

You say you want a threesome,

Your desires won't be dismissed,

Because what's better than one, my love?

But now TWO people pissed!

You say you want a threesome,

No matter what I say,

You don't even like gay people,

But I guess lesbians are okay!?!?!

You say you want a threesome,

And boy I aim to please.

So open your mouth real wide, my love,

And get on both your knees.

You say you want a threesome,

Cause that would be real fly,

I have no problem with that, my love,

As long as I can pick the guy.

Where Do You Find These Trash Men You Complain About On Facebook?

We find them at the grocery store,

We find them down the block,

We find them at our work stations,

Just trying to give us cock.

We find them at the hospital,

We find them when we're sick.

We find them at the funeral,

Just trying to give us dick.

We find them right here on the Earth,

We find them even on Venus.

We find them at the astrodome,

Just trying to give us penis.

We find them at your homeboy's house,

We find them at the gym,

We find them denying our experiences on Facebook,

Cause it looks like you are himmmmmmmmmm.

But You Claim You Don't See Patriarchy

Father, somewhere securing chasteness,

By pointing a gun in some prom date's face,

To insure his daughter doesn't wilt her flower,

While encouraging his son to overpower.

Father, with teenage girl locked in her room,

Key owned by him, given to her groom,

Will encourage his son to rock the world,

Of someone else's baby girl.

Father, somewhere policing her skirt,

While teaching his son how to flirt;

And teaching his daughter to be weary of boys' tactics,

While handing his son prophylactics.

Father, while keeping boys at bay,

Will teach his son, how to prey,

And protect his daughter from boys like his,

Because he knows firsthand that men ain't shit.

The Second Shift

We both worked forty hours this week,
You come home and barely speak..
You turn on the game to watch sweaty men,
While I slave hours in the kitchen.

You don't help me with the kids,
But want to practice having them.
I can't leave you alone with them for five minutes
which you call "babysitting."

You don't help me around the house,
"I," had to kill that fucking mouse.
You haven't washed a dish at all,
But want to go play basketball

You steadily talk about my weight,
while you go to the gym everyday.
I would like to work out too,
But I've got all this shit to do.

Sometimes I just need time to myself,

Like every fucking body else,

But I can't leave the house for an hour,

Without you calling my phone 'til it loses power.

You're always running out the door,

Without telling me what you're leaving for;

But let me look nice trying to leave the house

And all of a sudden, "I'M" the shitty spouse.

GLASShole CEILING

You are automatically smart,

But I always have to prove it,

Even though I have a masters,

And you almost flunked out of school.

You haven't a hint as how to do this job,

How are you even my superior?

But when it comes to intellect

Well, it's clear you are inferior.

Disguised as needing my input,

You will sit and pick my brain,

But when we're in board meetings,

You take credit for what I say.

Now, I understand as the boss,

You have to tell others what to do,

But why, when it comes to your own job,

You haven't the faintest clue?!?!?

The only thing you're good at,

Seems to be how to mansplain.

You talk over and for others,

time and time again.

What even are your qualifications?

The answer clearly lies,

It's not what's between your ears that matters,

But what's between your thighs,

Cause when I ask myself,

How'd you even get this gig?

It doesn't take a genius to figure out

Oh that's right, he has a dick.

Wedding Belles

Being happy is an accomplishment,

Not a marriage,

You can still have a fairytale life,

Without the horse and carriage.

Cause half of all marriages end in divorce,

And what's one person's destiny isn't yours.

A rock on finger does not secure,

A loving marriage that will endure.

And marriage does not a real woman make,

Cause sometimes the only thing sweet was the cake,

Little girls are taught that a prince will come and save the day

Instead of knowing how to pave their own way.

And if a happy wife means a happy life,

Then so many men likely won't survive.

The key to life is, good food, good sex, and laughter,

And that my darling, is your happily ever after.

I'm rich bitch

If I had a dollar for every sexual assault ,

I would be even richer,

Every time some dick

Said it was my fault.

If I had a quarter for every time someone told me to smile,

I could take the bus,

And not be subjected to

571 cat calls while walking just a mile.

If I had a dime for every time some guy was rude

I would have enough to buy some dick;

Cause sexual repression and not justified annoyance,

Is apparently the reason for my attitude.

If I had a nickel for every time some man made me uneasy,

I could have enough to hire someone

To say, "get the fuck outta her face, or else."

And men not think I'm teasing.

If I had a penny for every time some guy said something strange.

I could gather up all the money I've made,

Be rich as fuck,

And still nothing would ever change.

The "N" Word

Little girls are always informed,

To be a little lady

And smile real warm,

But if a male child seeks to destroy

Or make her cry,

that's just boys being boys

Little girls are always taught

That no one likes a girl,

Who acts like the boss.

So when you find yourself in sticky sitches

Remember to still be nice,

Cause no one likes bitches.

Little girls are often given the word

That children are to be seen

But not to be heard.

So when she's does just as she's told

Don't be surprised,

She didn't tell a soul.

Little girls aren't taught to defend themselves

Autonomy is a feeling

They've never felt,

So when a boy makes her uncomfortable

Don't be surprised

she doesn't know how to say "no."

It's My Prerogative

Some days I don't feel like dressing up,

Some days I just I want to get all made up,

Because it's my body and I can do what I want...

Every single day.

Some days I'm just not in the mood,

Some days all I wanna do is screw,

Because it's my body and I can do what I want...

Every single day

Some days I wanna dress like a hoe,

Some days I wanna dress like church folks,

Because it's my body and I can do what I want...

Every single day.

Some days I choose to have another kid,

Some days I choose an abortion,

Because it's my body and I can do what I want...

Every single day.

On no days do I have to change to suit your vision

On no days do I have to ask for your permission,

Because it's my body and I can do what I want,

And that's every single day!

Multitasking

It shouldn't be up for debate,

Of whether I should stay over my guy friend's house,

Or drive home real late.

Staying here doesn't seem like danger

But after a few drinks,

A good friend can quickly become stranger.

I shouldn't really have to think

If I can go to a bar,

And just enjoy my drink,

Because just one moment that I look up,

And someone could slip something,

Right in my cup.

I shouldn't have to sit and suppose,

whether a guy is genuinely nice

Or trying to get in my clothes.

whether he really is trying to help,

Or does he just want to help himself,

to a little something else.

I shouldn't have to be on guard,

when walking from my job.

Right to my car.

But being a woman isn't worry free.

Even though being a woman,

is the only thing I should have to be.

You Paying For Daycare, Hoe?

Please don't ask me why I don't have a son,

Could it be that I actually am not ready for one,

Please don't ask me why I don't have a son,

It's because I like to travel, and do cool shit, have a lot of fun,

Things that are hard to do with one.

Please don't ask me why I don't have a girl,

Maybe I'm too busy seeing the world.

Please don't ask me why I don't have a girl,

Just because I sit, slide, ride, on dick and do a twirl,

Doesn't mean I'm ready for my shell to produce a pearl.

Please don't ask my why I don't have kids,

Because a woman's worth is not connected to them,

Please don't ask me why I don't have kids,

I don't ask you if there is something wrong with your dick,

Fuck you, you little bitch!

Do you even like men?

I am not a monolith,

I am not one way.

So if I talk about men's shit

That doesn't mean I'm gay.

I am not a monolith,

I am not one way,

I can tell one dick to come,

And keep others at bay.

I am not a monolith,

I am not one way,

Cause when I speak of racism,

Black men have nothing to say.

I am not a monolith

I am not one way,

So if I talk on feminism,

That doesn't mean men I hate.

I am not a monolith,

I am not one way,

So don't ask me if I like men,

Please go the fuck away......the end.

From the Author

What originally started off as a Facebook status/tongue-in-cheek poem about where women find men who aren't of the highest caliber, if you will, soon went viral, and the idea to write a collection of poems about patriarchy, misogyny, and sexism, with an "elementary," approach, was born. I wanted to address serious concerns for many women, but in a comical way, but I struggled with how I would tackle certain issues, like rape and domestic violence, with the same light-hearted feel as the rest of the book, but still bring honor to the graveness of those situations. I had included more serious poems about infertility, but decided that they weren't suited for the feel of the project. Stylistically, the poems were a different writing style than what I am known for, but still have my voice and sense of humor.

I would like to dedicate this book to women who have supported me and aided my survival, women who have inspired me, women who have inspired others, as well as themselves. Women who had to choose between telling their stories and being made to survive another tragic one....no matter what decision they made....women who traded fire-starting stories with dragons.

I would like to thank my mother, an accidental feminist, who only takes shit when there's a diaper involved, and my dad, who taught me how to use these hands. I would like to thank Jay and Shon, for inspiring me to write, and perform, my closest friends who've always supported my poetry, Scott Woods, who mansplained me into writing this book, my high school German teacher Frau Moore (Gerber) who taught me so much about life in general, Dara for being so short, but yet so easy to look up to, Amir, the best poet in the universe, Casandra, my token friend, my mountain firefly, for being so hard to get over and lighting up my hands with wonder, Amy Winehouse for healing me in ways she may not have been able to do for herself, and my cats for not walking across my computer too much and deleting my manuscript; because what's a feminist without cats?!?!?!

About the Author

Kyla Jenée Lacey is an accomplished third person bio writer. She is also a pretty accomplished spoken word artist, whose poetry has been viewed millions of times on platforms like; Write About Now, George Takei, Afropunk, Occupy Democrats, Golden Mic TV, and All Def Digital. She has performed a one woman show of poetry, storytelling, and comedy, at over 200 colleges in over 40 states. She has written for the Huffington Post, The Root, and is a lover of the environment; even though she drinks bottled water. She is owned by two black cats, Kit and Kaboodle, and the not yet named cat whom she feeds, that lives on her porch. This is her first book, but lucky for you, this won't be her last; she's also ridiculously humble.

IG: KylaJLacey

Twiitter: KylaJLacey

Email:thatswriteKyla@gmail.com

Made in the USA
Las Vegas, NV
13 November 2024

11716593R00022